Behind Her Eyes

Zoie Jenkyns

Presentation by *BookLeaf Publishing*

Web: www.bookleafpub.com

E-mail: info@bookleafpub.com

ISBN: 9789395756952

First edition 2022

DEDICATION

This book is dedicated to anyone living with anxiety - you are not alone.

ACKNOWLEDGEMENT

I would like to take this opportunity to thank my partner, Alex. You have continuously supported and encouraged me to better understand my relationship with anxiety, and patiently stood by me through my highs and lows. Thank you for joining me on this rollercoaster, there's no one else I'd rather have by my side.

PREFACE

When I embarked on this journey, I didn't really know what to expect. I wanted to express and share my relationship with anxiety to those around me who sometimes don't always understand how I see or experience the world. I initially questioned whether many of these poems should be included as most can be difficult to read - however I began this journey as I didn't want to mask these experiences anymore, so I decided to share each and every one, in the hopes that they will provide others with insight and understanding to their own or others' relationship with anxiety.

Underneath

A single spotlight, the whole world is watching.
One wrong move and it will haunt you for the
rest of your nights.
A lifetime of rehearsing, you could perform
while sleeping,
but the performance is merely, life.

A roller coaster loops, your stomach drops,
your body thrown from side to side.
A combination of excitement and nausea,
but each day you're thrown on a new ride.

The jolting fright of a nightmare,
panicked and short of breath.
The exhaustion you can't remember,
It feels like you haven't slept.

Job interview intimidation,
silence fills the room.
Your stomach spinning like a washing machine,
It's like watching an old cartoon.

Combine those feelings together,
and play them on repeat,
welcome to a day in the life,
that's what's going on underneath.

Waking in the Unknown

Disguised in the crowds.
Hidden behind the smile, the laughter, the
picture perfect happiness.
Take a picture and you'll see a person who
belongs.

Underneath the surface.
Exhausted by the hurt, the confusion, the
constant battle.
Bruises left only on the inside.

Wanting, trying, hoping, desperate to fit in
amongst a crowd that already appears to accept
her for all that she is.
But they don't know who she is. At least not on
the inside.
And neither does she.

Lack of control, strings being pulled like a
puppet show on your own stage.
Strings being pulled by your own hands, your
hands being controlled by your mind. Your
MIND. YOUR mind.

The battle begins again. A war zone between
your mind and your mind. YOUR mind. Your
minds. Who will win?

A stranger to themselves, each day waking in the
unknown.

Supersonic Senses

When I am anxious, all my senses are
heightened;
everything is processed two-fold.
Everything is brighter, everything is bolder,
nothing quite fits it's mould.

The sounds are alarming, all of them at once,
yet I can tell each one apart.
And from meters away, if you whispered my
name,
I'd still hear it as sharp as a dart.

My tastebuds are bigger and more picky than
ever,
turning away at the mere sight.
Everything is hotter, everything is colder,
nothing seems to be "just right".

My nose starts to crinkle and crunch at all
smells,
both sweet ones and potent ones too.
They're not overwhelming and overpowering for
all,
but for me one small scent can cram a room.

One small touch can send me wailing,
unexpected, predicted or not.
While most people have specific areas to avoid,
my whole body is a sensitive spot.

Let's not forget about my emotions,
while they're not technically considered a
"sense".
But they too become heightened causing
overreactions,
to seemingly minor events.

When I am anxious I have supersonic senses,
making me extra alert.
I become very heightened, and quickly
frightened,
often appearing at my worst.

I'm Okay

I'm exhausted after sleeping.
I'm tired though I'm bright.
I'm laughing while I'm in pain.
I'm awake through the night.

I'm both guilty and I'm innocent.
I'm naked and I'm clothed.
I'm translucent but not transparent.
On the inside, no one knows.

I'm here but I'm also there.
I understand you but I don't.
I pretend that I'm okay,
so you don't make a mental note.

Further away than ever before,
but closer than here.
Don't whisper any secrets,
the echo will break my ear.

Weak

Lately, I've been taking the time that I need.
It's amazing, when I'm alone what I can achieve.
But some days, the sun doesn't shine as bright.
That's when, things don't feel so right.

I can get so weak sometimes,
something takes a hold of me,
and I lose all control of it.

Today's the day that I come clean.
I will fight it, with everything inside of me.
There's nothing I can do.
Except for tell you, that I am coming after you.

I can get so weak sometimes,
something takes a hold of me,
and I lose all control of it.

Low Battery

I wake from slumber tired and drowsy,
the mornings always have me feeling so lousy.

The alarm sirens, for the third time in a row,
My body starting to move, ever so slow.

I drag my feet out of bed, and into the cold,
I think morning people are ever so bold.

They gear up and move so effortlessly,
while I fight my eyes from returning to sleep.

The sun travels higher, warming the air,
I'm beginning to waken, the sun warming my
hair.

Quick! Only 5 minutes to be out the door,
I scurry my things, my time management is so
poor.

I'm running behind schedule and I've left things
behind,
I feel like I have so much on my mind.

I use all my energy to impress at my job,

How do people still find the time and energy to
jog?

I get home exhausted, not knowing what to do
first,
maybe the toilet before my bladder will burst.

Dinner and TV and I'm finally relaxed,
5 more minutes please, my brain needs that.

Consumed by distractions, now 11.00pm,
Time to go to bed and do it all over again.

Brain Vs. Reality

Excited beyond belief with butterflies in my
stomach;
Possibilities are endless, my mind racing wild.
Overjoyed with forethought and impulsive
goals,
Emotions flooding in by the pile.

Bursting at the seams, yet to be tamed,
A child on Christmas morning, jumping with
joy.
Heart racing fast and shortness of breath,
There's nothing that could possibly destroy.

"Don't get your hopes up", "Don't get ahead of
yourself",
Reality comes quickly crashing down.
Hopes and dreams already soaring,
I end up just feeling like the class clown.

Filled with disappointment and words of "it'll be
fine!",
Doesn't quite reach that same place.
Without any event, the rollercoaster was tiring,
Like my brain and reality just ran a race.

A Thoughtful Gift

She likes watching classic movies.
She likes dressing up.
She enjoys popular music.
So I gifted her tickets to a musical theatre.

But what if she doesn't like it? What if she's not
interested? What if she'd rather something else?

She loved it.

But what if she's just saying that? What if she
never wants to go again? What if it's the worst
gift I've ever given? What if she expected
something better? What if...

He likes crude humour.
He enjoys a pub meal.
He likes cracking a joke with the guys.
So I gifted him tickets to dinner and a comedy
show.

But what if he doesn't like it? What if he's not
interested? What if he'd rather something else?

He loved it.

But what if he's just saying that? What if he never wants to go again? What if it was the worst gift I've given? What if he expected something better? What if...

My Anxiety is My Superpower

My anxiety makes me overthink,
which can sometimes be a downfall.
But mostly it makes me care too much,
which isn't a bad thing at all.

My anxiety makes me avoid things,
which can sometimes make me miss out.
But mostly it makes me unexpectedly surprised,
when I enjoy something new without freaking
out.

My anxiety can be debilitating,
and can at times make me paralysed.
But mostly it makes me overexcited,
like a child experiencing things for the first time.

My anxiety can make me fixate,
on one thing for hours at a time.
But mostly it makes me strive for perfection,
which definitely keeps me in line.

My anxiety can be a lot to handle,
and at times makes me worse for wear.
But mostly it makes me who I am,
and it gives me my own flare.

Do you ever feel like you have anxiety?

Do you ever feel like you're being watched?
Like there's eyes on you constantly around the clock?

Do you ever feel like you're being criticized?
Like there's someone in the distance, squinting their eyes?

Do you ever feel like there's something lurking in the shadows?
Or like the walls are caving in, the corridor becoming narrow?

Do you ever feel like you're not good enough?
Like sometimes you may as well just give up?

Do you ever feel like tomorrow is too hard?
Like it's not even here yet but you've already put up your defense guard?

Do you ever feel like there's no escape?
Like no matter where you run, it's already too late?

Do you ever feel like you have anxiety?
Like it wasn't invited but still came to the party?

I'm Invited

There's a gathering tonight, I'm invited.
All my friends are going, and a bunch of people
I don't know.
What if I get stuck making small talk?
It's okay I'll just hide behind my phone.

But isn't the whole point of a gathering,
to mingle and socialise?
So why even bother going,
if I'm just going to hide.

There's a gathering tonight, I'm invited.
All my friends will be there.
So I can't wear the same thing I wore last time,
or else people may stare.

Perhaps I'll buy a new dress,
but what if someone is wearing the same thing?
They'll think I'm trying to be like them,
that would be so embarrassing.

But meeting all these social obligations,
seems impossible and unfair.
So why even bother going,
if I have nothing to wear?

There's a gathering tonight, I'm invited.
I'll need time for makeup and hair.
How do theirs always look so effortlessly
perfect?
Mine just never compares.

Three hours later and I still don't look,
the way I had intended.
So why even bother going,
if I'm going to be disappointed?

There's a gathering tonight, I'm invited.
What time should I arrive?
Fashionably late or early?
Irrelevant if they don't know I'm alive.

What if I arrive too late,
and miss out on all the mingling.
Everyone would already be in cliques,
and I would struggle to fit in.

What if I arrive too early,
and there's no one else in sight.
They'd think I was a dork,
are there worse ways to ruin a night?

But what if I arrive too late,
and everyone's on their way out.

So why even bother going,
if I'm just going to end up missing out.

There's a gathering tonight, I'm invited.
All my friends are going, and a bunch of people
I don't know.
There's a gathering tonight, I'm invited.
I'd simply rather not go.

Floating Ball

Picture a simple square,
trapped inside is a floating ball.
There's no gravity, it's moving freely,
bouncing from wall to wall.

Now imagine the walls are four big buttons,
triggering anxious thoughts.
Every time the ball hits a wall,
it triggers an anxiety response.

Many of my days are calm,
I float through time like the ball.
But then suddenly I feel anxious,
for absolutely no reason at all.

Somedays I move rapidly,
and I'm anxious all day long.
Sometimes I move so slow,
I barely feel anxious at all.

Ocean

Sitting on the bottom of the ocean floor,
I don't even know what I'm here for.
All I know is life is like the ocean,
Tides go up and down like emotions.

Everybody's talking about a time they were here.
But nobody knew 'cause they wanted to
disappear.

Riding down a wave with tunnel vision,
I've got no idea what I've got myself in.
Every time I close my eyes it's like,
My whole body's on fire but fighting with ice.

Everybody's talking about the size of the wave.
Was it big enough or do they think that I just
caved?

The water is always moving.
The tides are always changing.
Sometimes it pulls you under, and you can't
breathe.

The water is always moving.
The tides are always changing.

Sometimes you get caught in a rip out to sea.

Now I'm floating,
on the surface of the ocean.
Would anybody find me?
Would anybody know?

Battlefield

Living with anxiety is like living in a battlefield. You're always on edge, always expecting the worst, and never knowing if you're about to step on a land mine.

The ground is unsteady, and it's often difficult to find your "rock" or your "centre" for stability. Instead, you look to other means: an object, a routine, or anything familiar that brings comfort and peace of mind; something to rely on.

The only problem? When that object is lost or broken, or when that routine is changed.

When the unexpected happens, you don't know what to expect next. You no longer have stability. You no longer feel comfort.

You become scared.
You become defensive.
You become irrational.
You become impulsive.
You become emotional.
You become reckless.
You become, the battlefield.

ANXIOUS

A is for Always Agonising over things that don't matter.
N is for Never saying No to others.
X is for eXaggerating every possible outcome.
I is for Insecure thoughts.
O is for Overthinking every scenario.
U is for Undermining yourself.
S is for always saying Sorry.

Fight. Flight. Fright.

I wouldn't consider myself a runner,
or even fit to run a race.
But I often find myself fleeing a scene,
when a challenge presents to my face.

I wouldn't consider myself harmful,
I wouldn't hurt a fly.
But often I'm the one throwing hurtful words,
Ready to put up a fight.

I wouldn't consider myself scared,
or even timid or shy.
But I often become frozen,
and have been known to even hide.

I wouldn't usually describe myself,
with any of the above.
But anxiety often makes me respond,
in ways that I'm not proud of.

Innocent Victims

Inconvenient and unwelcome lies the monster
inside;
defeat-able though not destructible.
Insightful eyes, but full of lies,
it makes you question your own.

Subtle and somber it lurks deep within;
most completely unaware.
So obvious and true, to the ones who already
knew,
perhaps it is time to share.

Strong and heavy the burden resides,
in the bottomless pit of despair.
Refraining from telling, while considerably
relieving,
would be deemed as quite unfair.

Big and small, weak and strong,
it's victims have no common theme.
It will drain you and change you, but don't let it
control you,
once you know, you can be free.

Unknown

In times of uncertainty, I look for solid ground.
I become repetitive and predictable.
I rely on what I know to be true,
and what I know cannot be changed.

I re-watch the same movie because knowing
how it ends provides comfort;
I reflect on favourite memories because they are
replayed the same way;
I over-plan and over-prepare for what lies ahead;
Because I simply can't handle the unknown.

"I have anxiety"

Anxiety is just stress,
so stop stressing about your day.
Anxiety is all in your head,
just simply make it go away.

You're such a drama queen,
you're exaggerating this time.
Why are you overreacting?
everything is fine.

You always say you're tired,
you need to take more time to rest.
You always say you have no time for a break,
but you do, you just need to invest.

You need to be more active,
and take better care of your health.
But wait let me guess you've got none left,
no more energy to look after yourself.

It sounds like more excuses,
and now you've begun avoiding me.
I just don't understand you,
when you say, "I have anxiety".

What If...

What if the weather changes? What if we can't
go?
What if we can't even try again tomorrow?
What if we're late? What if we miss out?
What if it's gone, how will we figure that out?
What if it's different? What if it's changed?
What if it's never ever the same?
What if there's none left? What if it was the last
one?
What will we use to replace what's now gone?
What if they don't like it? What if they're not a
fan?
What if they don't want me to ever make another
plan?
What if I make a mistake? What if I fall?
What if they don't even notice me at all?
What if they forget me? What if they don't care?
What if I'm left with nothing but despair?
What if...

Behind My Eyes

When I do something incorrect, it crushes my
world,
I am always my most brutal critic.
I don't need you to highlight, all my flaws in the
spotlight,
I just need you to be there when I need it.

When you raise your voice, it makes me
crumble,
I can't handle that kind of attack.
It's demeaning, controlling and also belittling,
You can say what you need, but not like that.

I don't respond well to feedback or notes of
improvement,
I'm known to be quite defensive.
Because by the time you approach, you're the
100th coach,
my 99 prior thoughts quite pensive.

Not to mention my need for perfection,
it's not easy making mistakes.
But for others to notice, I'm not sure if you know
this,
my heart quite literally breaks.

Vulnerable now more than ever before,
you've probably never realised.
Always masked with composure, I don't like
exposure,
except now, you've seen a glimpse behind my
eyes.

www.ingramcontent.com/pod-product-compliance
Lightning Source LLC
Chambersburg PA
CBHW060922130726
48001CB00006B/2373